BIOGRAP DOLLY PARTON

Memoir, History and Achievements

COREY PARK

COPYRIGHT © Corey Park

All Rights Reserved

TABLE OF CONTENT

CHILDHOOD

PERSONAL LIFE

CAREER

AWARDS & NOMINATIONS

CONCLUSION

CHILDHOOD

Dolly Parton was born 1946 January 19 in a single room on the water's edge of the Little Pigeon River in Pittman Center, Tennessee. She is the fourth of Avie Lee Caroline and Robert Lee Par's twelve children. In 2021, Parton had three siblings that have died. Rebecca Whitted, Parton's maternal grandmother, is the inspiration for her middle name. Her dad worked in the mountains of East Tennessee, first as a tenant farmer and later tending his little tobacco homestead and grounds. Furthermore, he maintained development sources of income to enhance the ranch's little pay. Despite her father's illiteracy, Parton had said that he was one of the most brilliant persons she had ever met regarding business and profit.

Avie Lee, Parton's mother, took care of their huge family, where she had pregnant 11 times giving birth to one twin. Parton always praised her musical abilities to her mother; even though she was in poor health, she still managed to keep house and entertain her children with Smoky Mountain folklore and ancient ballads. Parton's mother's family hailed from Wales and sang the old songs of the immigrants who had moved to southern Appalachia over a century earlier. Avie Lee's father was a Pentecostal preacher, and Parton and her kin went to chapel routinely. Parton has long credited her dad for her business canny and her mom's family for her melodic capacities. Whenever Parton was a little child, her family moved from the Pittman Center region to a homestead close to Locust Ridge. Today, a big chunk of her cherished childhood memories took place there.

Dollywood, Dolly Parton's theme park, has a reproduction of the Locust Ridge cabin. The farm acreage and surrounding woodland inspired her to write the song My Tennessee Mountain Home in the 1970s. Parton repurchased the farm in the late 1980s, years after being sold. Bobby, her brother, assisted with the restoration and new construction of the building. She has portrayed her family as being down and out while her dad paid the specialist, who conveyed her with a pack of cornmeal. Parton and her family lived in their natural, one-room lodge on their little means ranch on Locust Ridge for six or seven years. This was a predominantly Pentecostal area north of the Great Smoky Mountains' Greenbrier Valley. As a child, music played an essential role in her life. In an assembly her grandpa, Jake Robert Owens, pastored, Dolly was brought up in the Church of God, Cleveland. Her earliest open exhibitions were in the congregation, starting at age six. At seven, she began playing a natively constructed guitar; her uncle bought her first real guitar at eight. Parton began her career as a child, singing on the radio. At ten, she was on WIVK Radio and WBIR-TV in Knoxville, Tennessee, on The Cas Walker Show. At 13, she recorded the single Puppy Love on a small Louisiana label, Goldband Records, and appeared at the Grand Ole Opry, where she first met Johnny Cash. He encouraged her to follow her instincts regarding her career.

Parton traveled to Nashville the next day after graduating from Sevier County High School in 1964. Shortly after arriving, her first big break came when she signed with Combine Publishing; she composed numerous singles with her frequent songwriting partner, Bill Owens (her uncle), including two Top 10 hits: Bill Phillips' Put It Off

Until Tomorrow and Skeeter Davis' Fuel to the Flame. During this time, numerous other performers, like Kitty Wells and Hank Williams Jr., recorded her songs. At 19, she was endorsed by Monument Records and was first pitched as a bubblegum pop vocalist. Despite her wish to record country music, Monument refused, believing that her distinctive high soprano voice was unsuited to the genre. After her composition, Put It Off Until Tomorrow, as recorded by Bill Phillips, went to number six on the country chart in 1966, the label relented and allowed her to record country. Her first country single, Dumb Blonde (composed by Curly Putman, one of the few songs during this era that she recorded but did not write), reached number 24 on the country chart in 1967, followed by Something Fishy, which went to number 17. The two songs appeared on her first full-length album, Hello, I'm Dolly.

PERSONAL LIFE

Parton is the fourth in a family of twelve children. Willadeene, David Wilburn, Coy Denver, Robert Lee, Stella Mae, Cassie Nan, Randle Huston (dead), Larry Gerald (deceased), Floyd Estel and Frieda Estelle twins, and Rachel Ann are her siblings.

Parton married Carl Thomas Dean, born on July 20, 1942, in Nashville, Tennessee, on May 30, 1966, in Ringgold, Georgia. Even though Parton doesn't utilize Dean's last name expertly, she has stated that her passport reads Dolly Parton Dean and sometimes uses Dean when signing contracts. Dean resigned from maintaining a black-top street clearing business in Nashville, has consistently disregarded exposure, and seldom goes with his better half. Parton and her husband announced on May 6, 2016, that they would renew their vows in honor of their 50th wedding anniversary later that month.

The couple had no children because she had endometriosis, which eventually led her to have a hysterectomy. Miley Cyrus, a singer and actress is Parton's goddaughter.

CAREER

Dolly started her career at a young age, and she ventures into music, songwriting, acting, and production.

In 1967 dolly patron began her music career. A musician and country music singer, Porter Wagoner, urged Parton to join his organization, promising her a weekly slot on his syndicated television show The Porter Wagoner Show and a spot on his roadshow. Much of Wagoner's audience was initially disgruntled that Norma Jean, the performer that Parton had replaced, had departed the program, as chronicled in her 1994 autobiography, and was hesitant to embrace Parton. With Wagoner's help, nonetheless, Parton was ultimately acknowledged. Wagoner was able to persuade RCA Victor to sign her. RCA decided to safeguard their speculation by delivering her most memorable single as a two-part harmony with Wagoner. That tune, a change of Tom Paxton's The Last Thing on My Mind, delivered in late 1967, arrived at the nation's Top 10 in January 1968, sending off a six-year dash of practically continuous Top 10 singles for the pair. Parton's most memorable performance single for RCA Victor, Just Because I'm a Woman, was delivered in 1968 and was a moderate outline hit, arriving at number 17. For the following two years, none of her independent endeavors - even In the Good Old Days (When Times Were Bad), which later turned into a norm - were as effective as her two-part harmonies with Wagoner. The Country Music Association named the duo Vocal Group of the Year in 1968, but Parton's solo records were continually ignored. Wagoner had a substantial financial stake in Parton's career; he was her co-producer and owned about half of Owe-Par, the publishing business she co-founded with Bill Owens, as of 1969.

In her pop transition between 1976 and 1986, Parton had a string of country hits between 1974 and 1980, with eight singles hitting number one. Many mainstream and crossover singers, including Olivia Newton-John, Emmylou Harris, and Linda Ronstadt, have covered her songs, demonstrating her influence on pop culture.

Parton initiated a high-profile crossover push to broaden the appeal of her music and raise her exposure outside of country music's limits. Sandy Gallin, who remained as her manager for the following 25 years, began working with her in 1976. Parton began taking a more active role in creating her 1976 album All I Can Do, which she co-produced with Porter Wagoner and began intentionally targeting her music in a more mainstream, pop direction. Her first entirely self-produced effort, the new harvest gathering, highlighted her pop sensibilities, both in terms of choice of songs. Though the album was well received and topped the U.S. country albums chart, neither its single Light of a Clear Blue Morning made much of an impression on the pop charts. Parton resorted to high-profile pop producer Gary Klein for her next album after New Harvest's poor crossover performance. Here You Come Again, released in 1977, was her first million-selling album, debuting at number one on the country album list and number 20 on the mainstream chart. Until the ending 1970s and mid-1980s, large numbers of her next singles, all the while climbed on the two outlines. Her collections during this period were grown explicitly for pop-hybrid achievement. Her album sales were still relatively robust in the mid-

1980s, with Save the Last Dance for Me, Downtown, Tennessee Homesick Blues in 1984, Real Love, Don't Call It Love in 1985, and Think About Love (1986) all reaching the country's Top 10. However, once her contract with RCA Records expired in 1986, she signed with Columbia Records in 1987.

From 1987 to 2005, Patron released a series of bluegrass-inspired albums, including the grass, is blue, which later won a Grammy award for best bluegrass albums, trim grass, halos & horns.

Parton is a prolific composer who began penning country music songs with folk elements based on her upbringing in the mountains and reflecting her family's Christian heritage. Her hits include Coat of Many Colors, I Will Always Love You, and Jolene. Parton was named a BMI Icon at the 2003 BMI Country Awards on November 4, 2003. Over 35

BMI Pop and Country Awards have been bestowed upon Parton. She was chosen for the Songwriters Hall of Fame in 2001. Parton has stated that she composes something every day, whether a song or an idea. Parton's songwriting has been utilized in several movies. She recorded a second version of I Will Always Love You for The Best Little Whorehouse in Texas, in addition to the title song for 9 to 5. The second version was a country success, charted at 53 in the pop charts. Whitney Houston sang it on the soundtrack for The Bodyguard. Her rendition turned into the top-rated hit composed and performed by a female singer, with more than twelve million duplicates overall. Likewise, the tune has been converted into Italian and performed by the Welsh drama vocalist Katherine Jenkins.

Parton and Sandy Gallin, her former manager, were co-owners of Sandollar Productions. It is a film and television production company that created Common Threads:

- Stories from the Quilt in 1989 later won an academy award for documentary.
- The television series Babes and Buffy the Vampire Slayer.
- The feature films Father of the Bride, Father of the Bride: Part II, Straight Talk in which Parton starred, and Sabrina 1995, among other shows.

Parton had television roles in addition to her performance appearances on The Porter Wagoner Show in the 1960s and 1970s, her two self-titled television variety series and American Idol in 2008, and numerous guest appearances. In 1979, she was nominated for an Emmy Award for Outstanding

Supporting Actress in a Variety Program for her guest appearance in a Cher special. During the mid-1970s, Parton wanted to expand her audience base. Her first attempt, the television variety show Dolly, received positive reviews but only lasted one season. Because of the strain on her vocal cords, Parton wanted to be released from her contract. Parton is featured close by Jane Fonda and Lily Tomlin in the comedy flick 9 to 5 as a secretary in her first major film. The film raises awareness for the National Association of Working Women by highlighting workplace discrimination against women.

AWARDS AND NOMINATIONS

Dolly Parton is widely recognized as one of the all-time great female country singers. 25 of her single or album releases have been certified as Gold, Platinum, or Multi-Platinum by the Record Industry Association of America. She has 26 songs that have charted at number one on the Billboard country charts, which is a record for a female singer. She has 42 vocation Top 10 country collections, a record for any craftsman, and 110 profession outlined singles throughout recent years. Starting around 2012, she had composed more than 3,000 melodies and sold more than 100 million records. She had topped the country music charts in each of the seven decades by 2021, the most of any singer.

Dolly Parton has received eleven Grammy Awards (including the Lifetime Achievement Award in 2011) and fifty Grammy Award nominations, making her the second-most nominated female performer in Grammy history. She received three awards out of 18 nominations at the American Music Awards. She has ten awards from 42 nominations from the Country Music Association. She has received seven wins and 39 nominations from the Academy of Country Music. Dolly is one of six female artists to win the Country Music Association's highest honor, Entertainer of the Year. She was also nominated for two Academy Awards, a Tony Award, and an Emmy Award for her appearance in a 1978 Cher television special. In 1984, she was honored with a star on the Hollywood Walk of Fame, located at 6712 Hollywood Boulevard in Hollywood, California; a star on the Nashville StarWalk for Grammy winners; and a bronze sculpture on the Sevierville courthouse yard. In 1969, Dolly Parton was admitted into the Grand Ole Opry, and she was named one of Ms. Magazine's Women of the Year in 1986. In 2005, she was honored with the National Medal of Arts, the highest honor given by the U.S. government for excellence in the arts, where the U.S. President presented the award. On December 3, 2006, Parton received the Kennedy Center Honors from the John F. Kennedy Center for the Performing Arts for her lifetime of contributions to the arts.

Some of country music's biggest names came to show their admiration during the show. On November 16, 2010, Parton accepted the Liseberg Applause Award, the theme park industry's most prestigious honor, on behalf of Dollywood theme park during a ceremony held at IAAPA Attractions

Expo 2010 Orlando, Florida. In 2015, a newly discovered species of lichen found growing in the southern Appalachians were named Japewiella dollypartoniana in honor of Parton's music and her efforts to bring national and global attention to that region. In 2018, Parton received a second star on the Hollywood Walk of Fame, inducted alongside Linda Ronstadt and Emmylou Harris to recognize their work as a trio. Parton was also recognized in the Guinness World Records 2018 Edition for holding records for the Most Decades with a Top 20 hit on Billboard's Hot Country Songs Chart and Most Hits on Billboard's Hot Country Songs Chart by a Female Artist. In 2020, Parton received a Grammy award for her collaboration with For King & Country on their song, God Only Knows. Due to her husband's condition and the ongoing pandemic, Parton has declined the Presidential Medal of Freedom twice.

CONCLUSION

Parton invested much of her earnings into her native East Tennessee business ventures, notably pigeon forge. She is a co-owner of the Dollywood company, which operates the theme park Dollywood, a dinner theater, Dolly Parton's stampede, the waterpark Dollywood splash country, and the Dream More Resort, and Spa, all in Pigeon Forge. Dollywood is the 24th-most-popular theme park in the United States, with three million visitors.

Parton's Dollywood Foundation has sponsored various charity endeavors, particularly in literacy. Her literacy program, Dolly Parton's Imagination Library, a part of the Dollywood Foundation, mails one book per month to each enrolled child from birth until they enter kindergarten. Over 1600 local communities throughout the United States, Canada, the United Kingdom, Australia, and the Republic of Ireland distribute the Imagination Library to around 850,000 children each month. In response to the COVID-19 pandemic, Parton donated $1 million towards research at Vanderbilt University Medical Centre and encouraged those who could afford it to make similar donations.

Printed in Great Britain
by Amazon